HOW TO DRAW Animals FOR KIDS

A STEP-BY-STEP GUIDE TO DRAWING

50+

DELIGHTFUL ANIMALS

This book belongs to:

____

TIPS FOR USING THIS BOOK

1. DRAW LIGHTLY AT FIRST USING A PENCIL - YOU MIGHT NEED TO ERASE SOME LINES ALONG THE WAY.

2. DRAW THE BLACK LINES IN EACH STEP AND TAKE YOUR TIME. DON'T WORRY IF YOUR ANIMAL DOESN'T LOOK EXACTLY LIKE THE ONE IN THIS BOOK. NO TWO ANIMALS ARE EVER EXACTLY THE SAME.. EVEN IN REAL LIFE!

3. GO BACK AND DARKEN YOUR FINAL LINES, THEN ADD SOME DETAILS AND COLOR IN YOUR NEW ANIMAL FRIEND! USE YOUR IMAGINATION AND MAKE IT YOUR OWN! MAYBE YOU WANT TO GIVE YOUR TIGER POLKA DOTS INSTEAD OF STRIPES!

4. KEEP PRACTICING AND HAVING FUN AND YOU WILL GET BETTER EACH TIME!

How to Draw Animals for Kids: A Step-by-Step Guide to Drawing 50+ Delightful Animals

TABLE OF CONTENTS

PETS

FARM ANIMALS

FOREST ANIMALS

JUNGLE ANIMALS

GRASSLAND ANIMALS

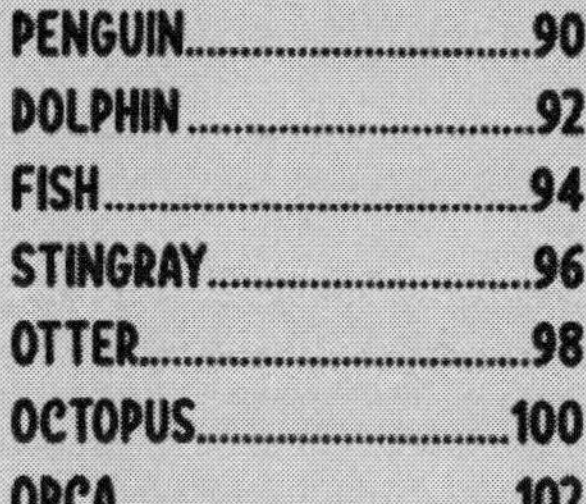

OCEAN ANIMALS

Cat

Step-by-step instructions

1

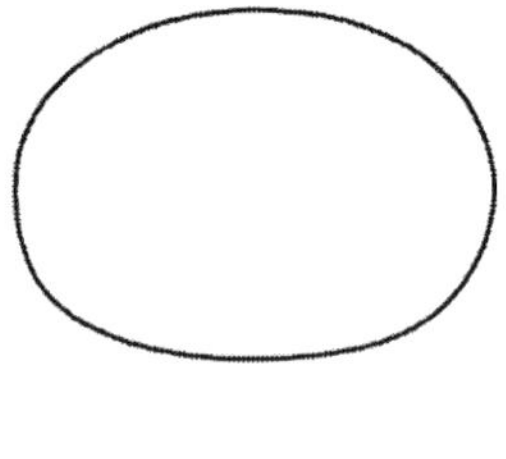

2

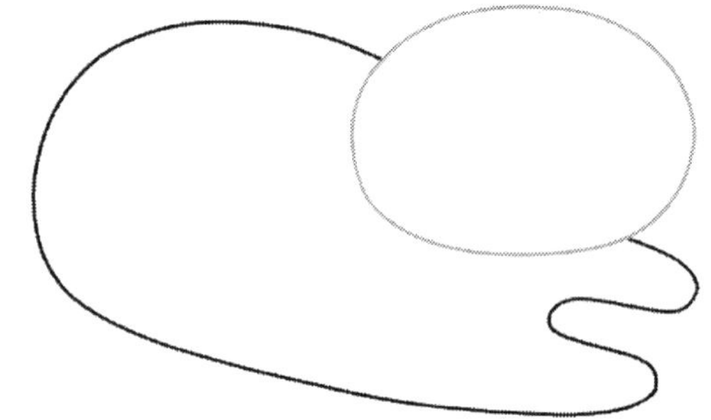

3

4

Trace along with me to practice

Now it's your turn on your own!

Turtle

Step-by-step instructions

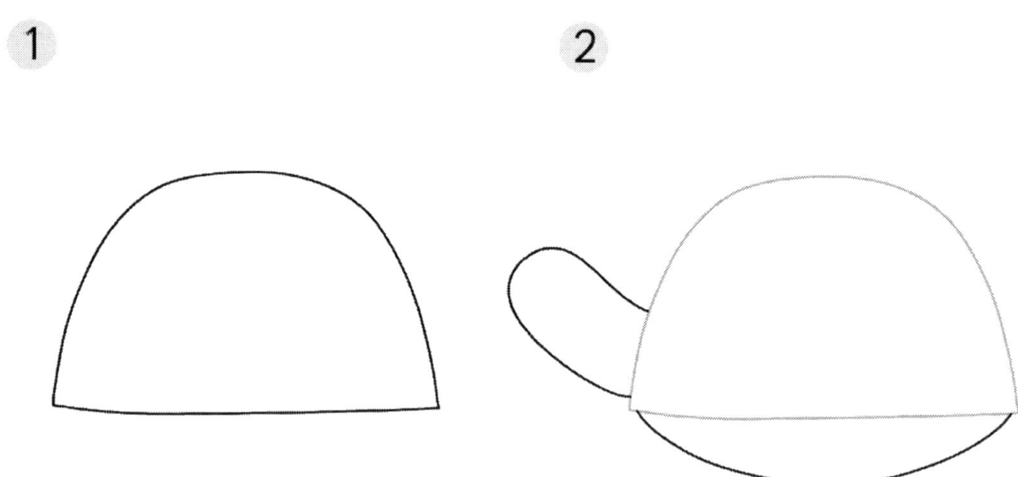

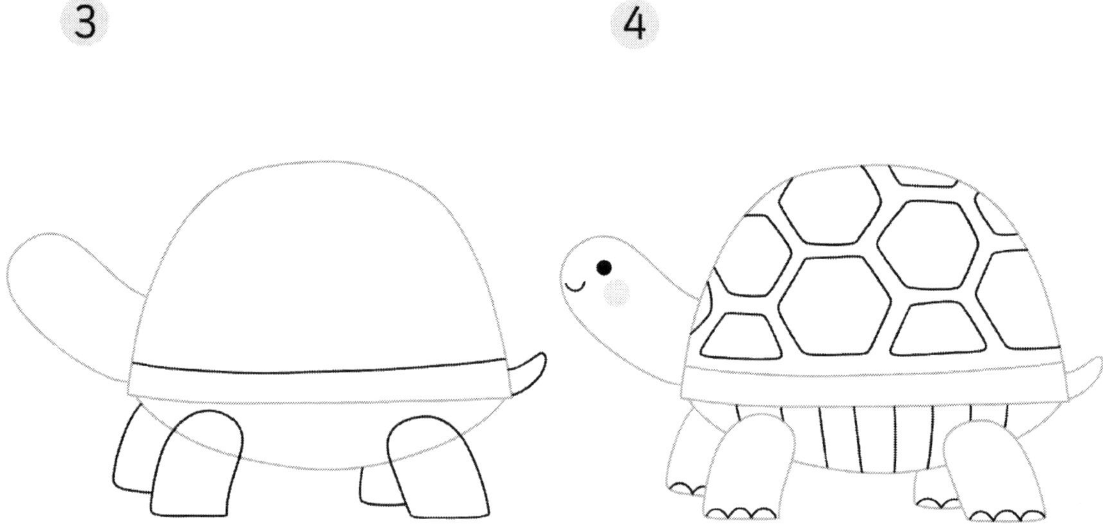

Trace along with me to practice

Now it's your turn on your own!

Dog

Step-by-step instructions

1

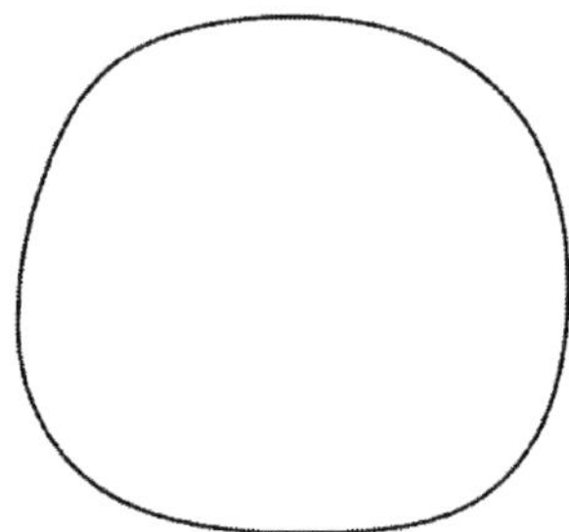

2

3

4

Trace along with me to practice

Now it's your turn on your own!

Bunny

Step-by-step instructions

1

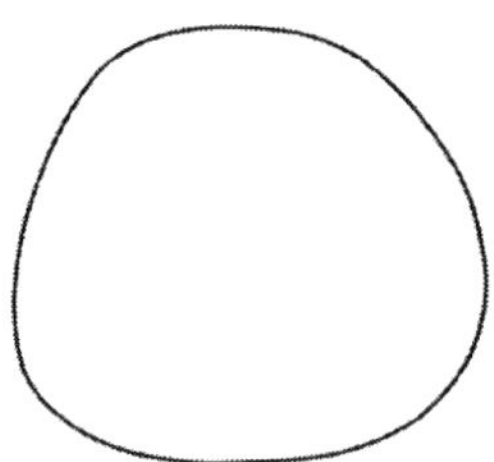

2

3

4

Trace along with me to practice

Now it's your turn on your own!

Hamster

Step-by-step instructions

1

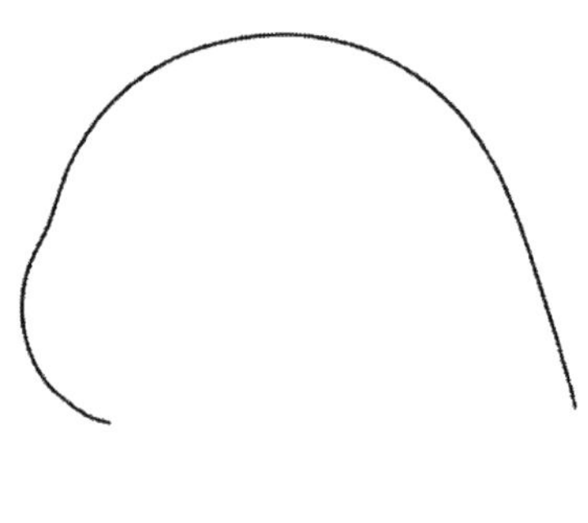

2

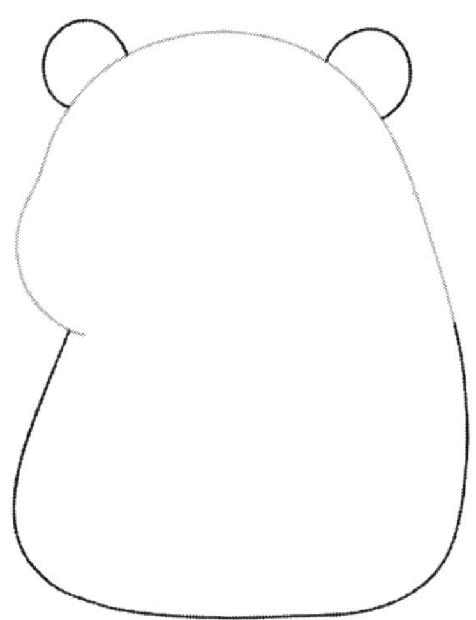

3

4

Trace along with me to practice

Now it's your turn on your own!

Mouse

Step-by-step instructions

1

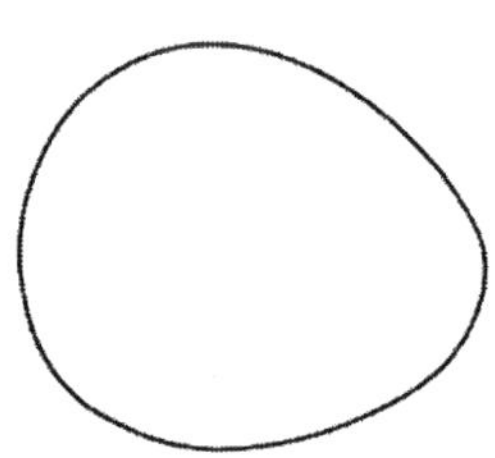

2

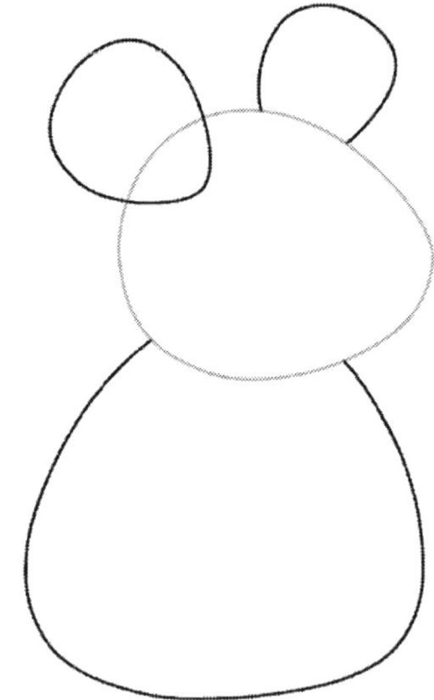

3

4

Trace along with me to practice

Now it's your turn on your own!

Cow

Step-by-step instructions

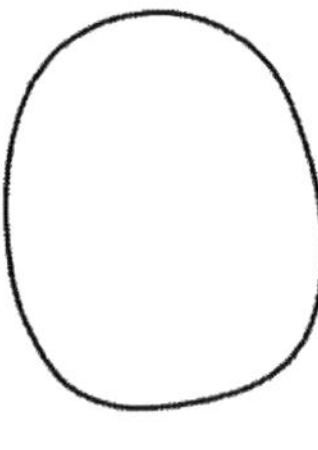

3

Trace along with me to practice

Now it's your turn on your own!

Chicken

Step-by-step instructions

1

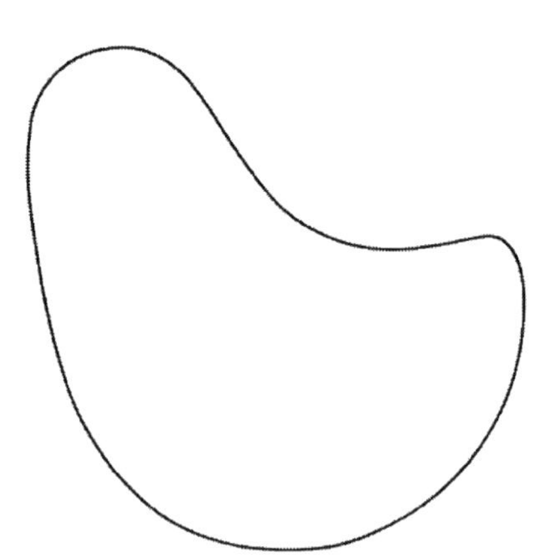

2

3

4

Trace along with me to practice

Now it's your turn on your own!

Horse

Step-by-step instructions

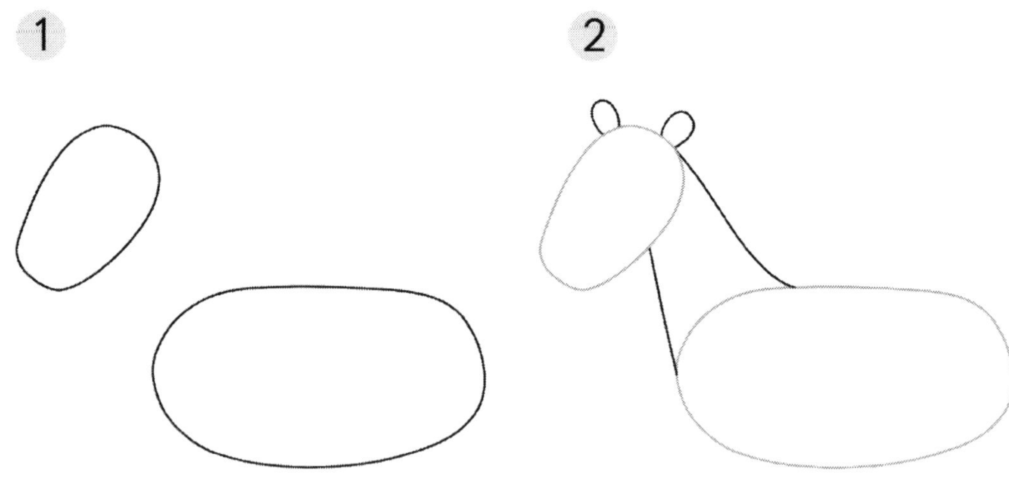

Trace along with me to practice

Now it's your turn on your own!

Llama

Step-by-step instructions

2

3

4

Trace along with me to practice

Now it's your turn on your own!

Goat

Step-by-step instructions

1

2

Trace along with me to practice

Now it's your turn on your own!

Pig

Step-by-step instructions

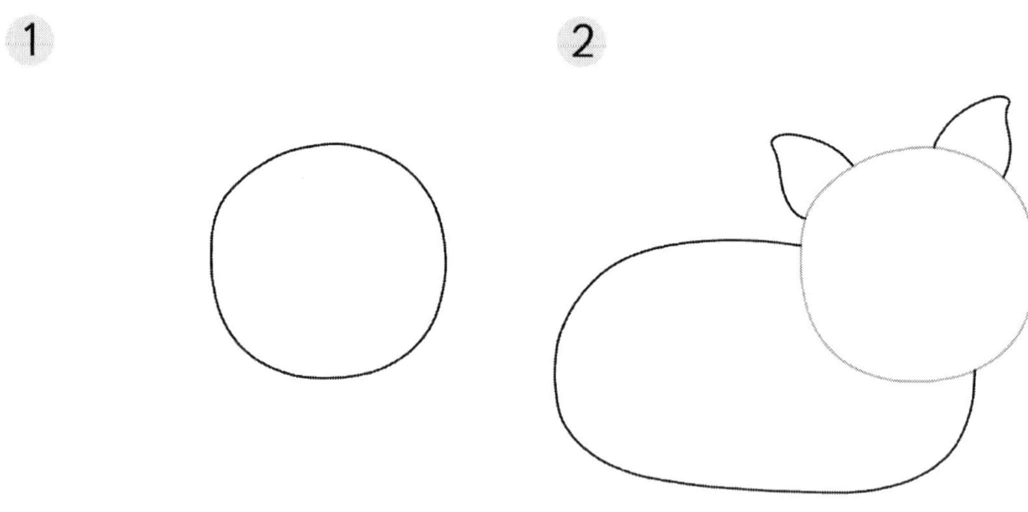

Trace along with me to practice

Now it's your turn on your own!

Sheep

Step-by-step instructions

1

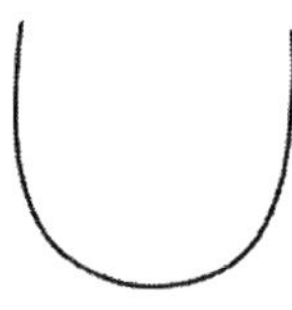

2

3

4

Trace along with me to practice

Now it's your turn on your own!

Donkey

Step-by-step instructions

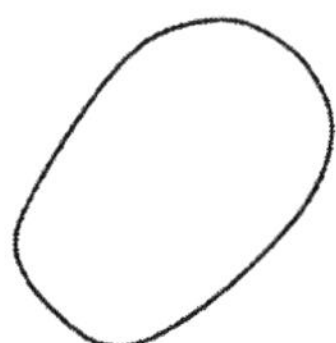

Trace along with me to practice

Now it's your turn on your own!

Duck

Step-by-step instructions

1

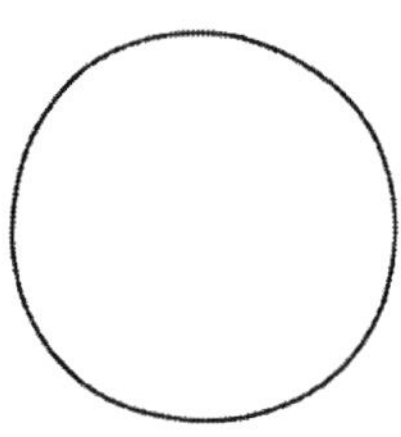

2

3

4

Trace along with me to practice

Now it's your turn on your own!

Deer

Step-by-step instructions

Trace along with me to practice

Now it's your turn on your own!

Bear

Step-by-step instructions

1

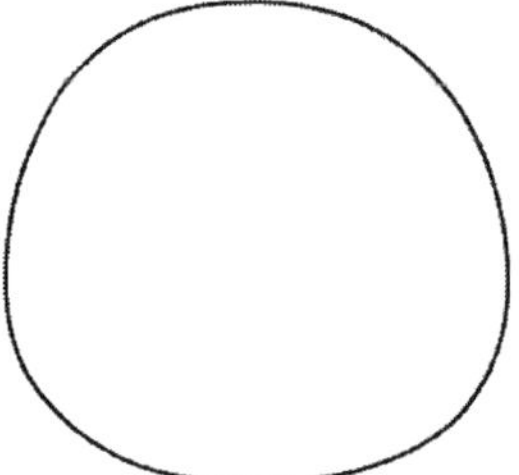

2

3

4

Trace along with me to practice

Now it's your turn on your own!

Fox

Step-by-step instructions

1

2

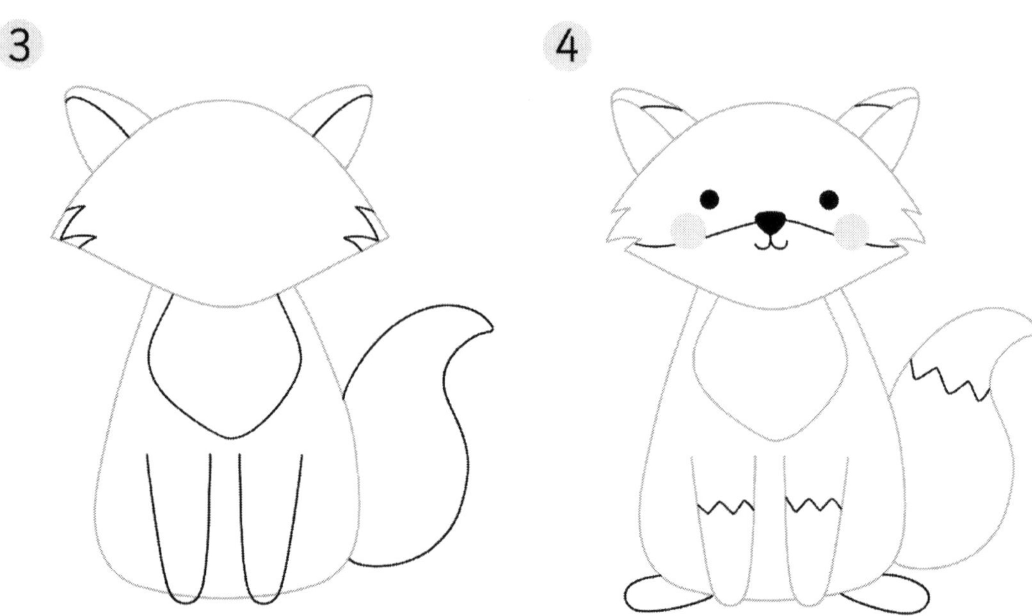

Trace along with me to practice

Now it's your turn on your own!

Hedgehog

Step-by-step instructions

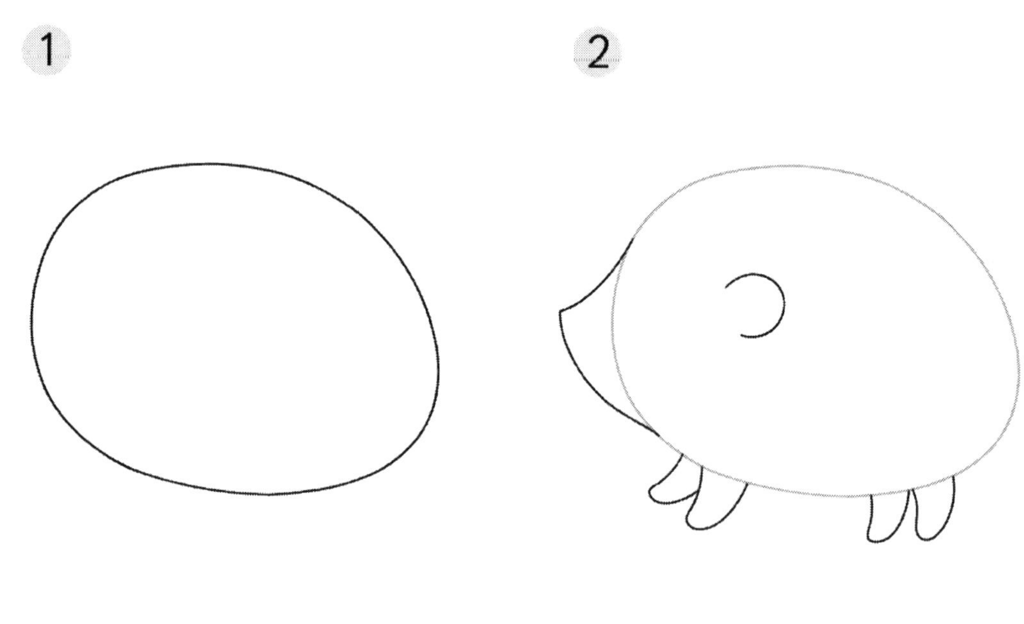

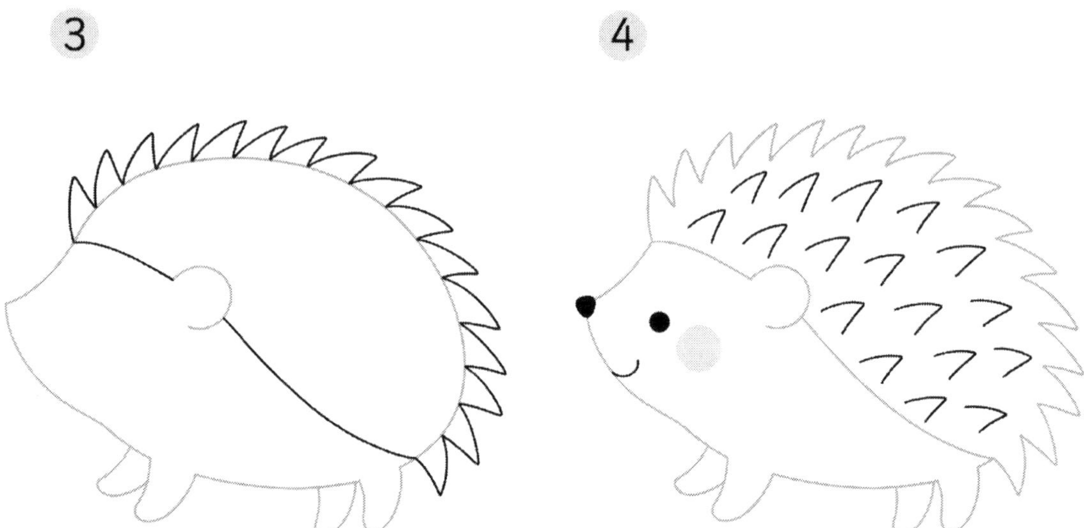

Trace along with me to practice

Now it's your turn on your own!

Raccoon

Step-by-step instructions

1

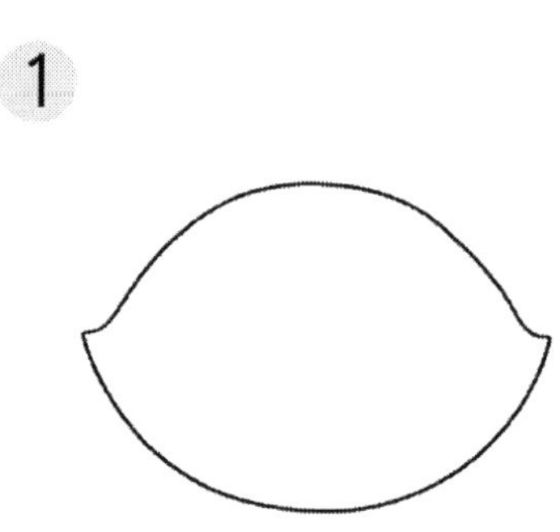

2

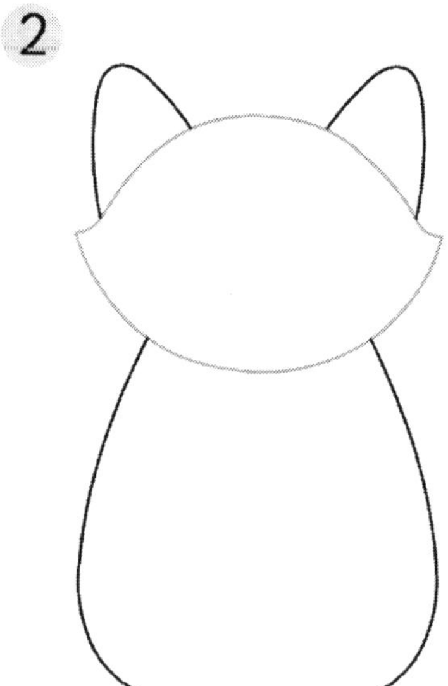

3

4

Trace along with me to practice

Now it's your turn on your own!

Owl

Step-by-step instructions

1

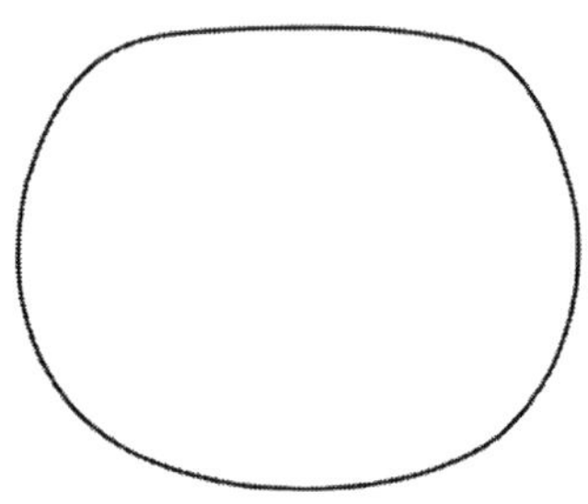

2

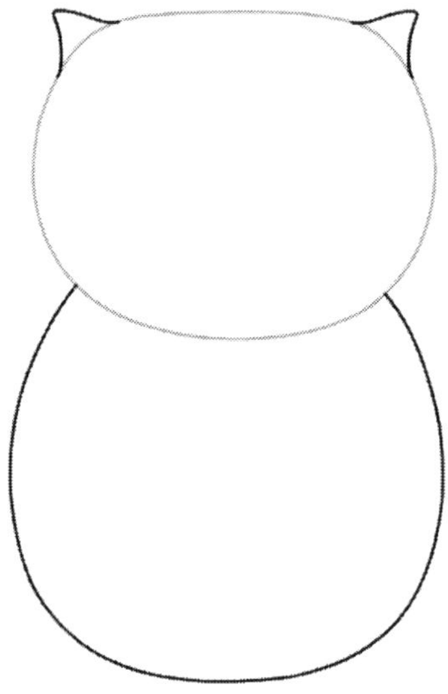

3

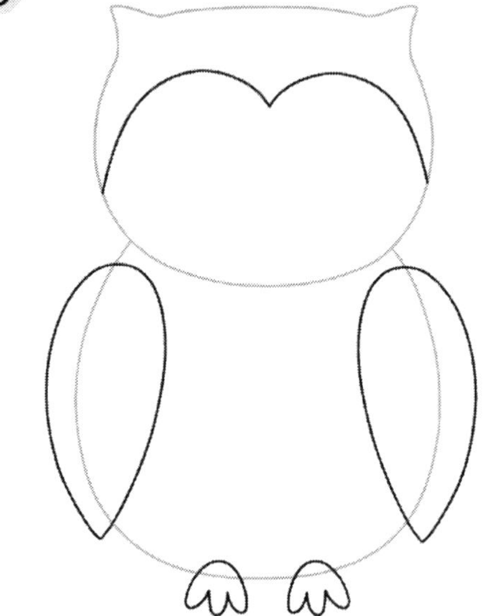

4

Trace along with me to practice

Now it's your turn on your own!

Skunk

Step-by-step instructions

1 2

3 4

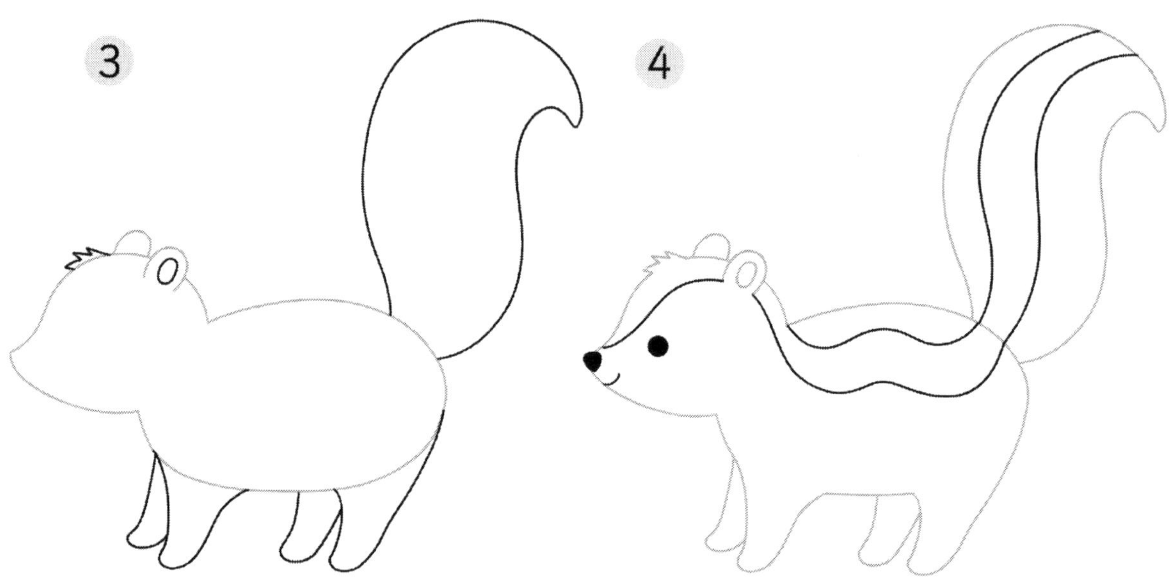

Trace along with me to practice

Now it's your turn on your own!

Moose

Step-by-step instructions

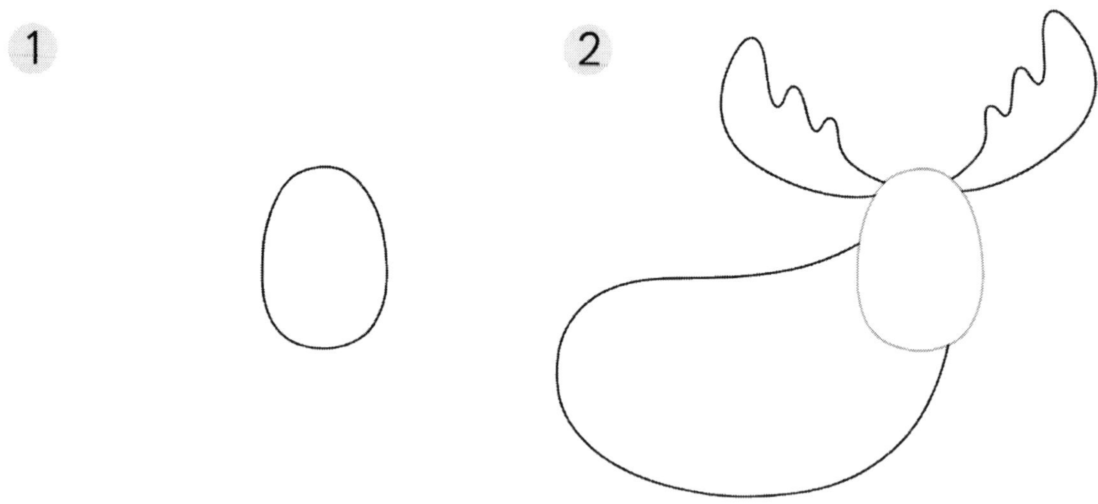

Trace along with me to practice

Now it's your turn on your own!

Squirrel

Step-by-step instructions

1

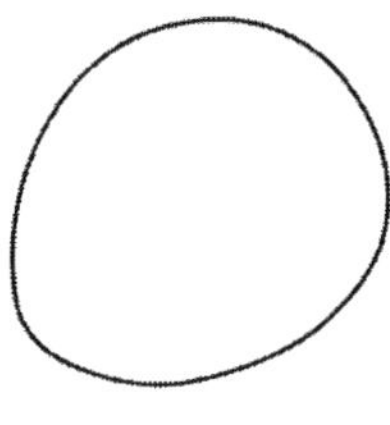

2

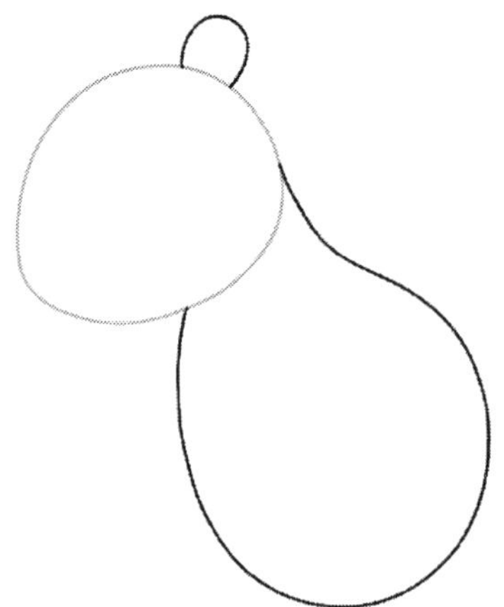

3

4

Trace along with me to practice

Now it's your turn on your own!

Tiger

Step-by-step instructions

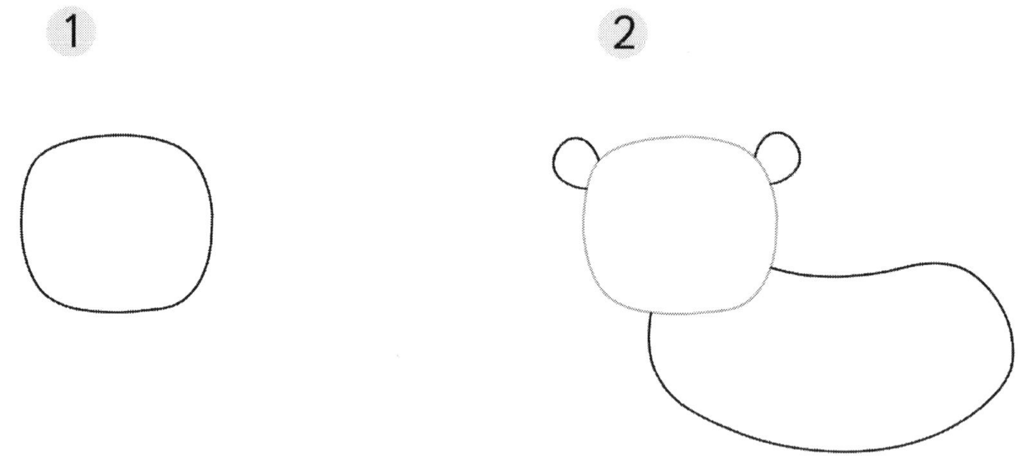

Trace along with me to practice

Now it's your turn on your own!

Monkey

Step-by-step instructions

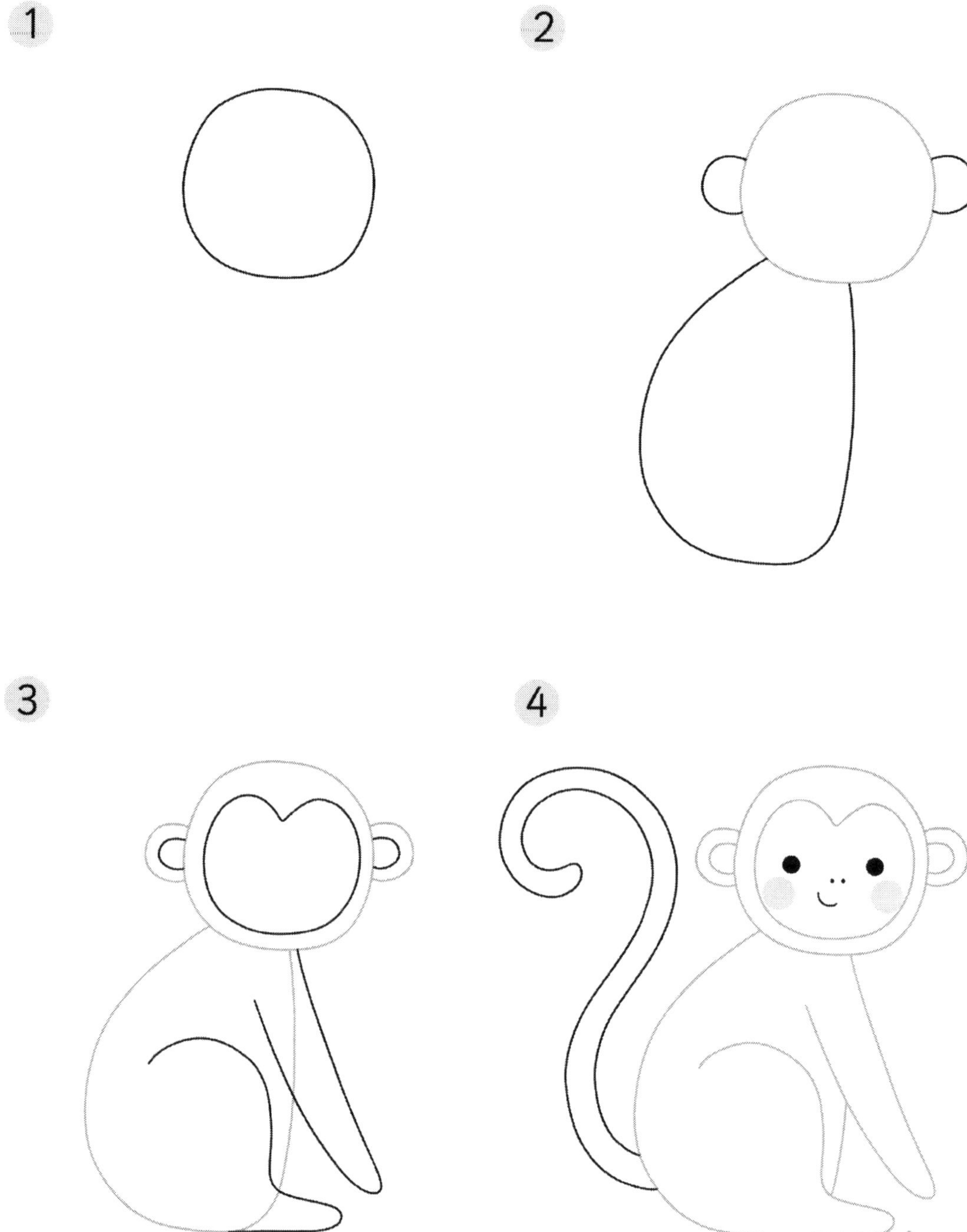

Trace along with me to practice

Now it's your turn on your own!

Sloth

Step-by-step instructions

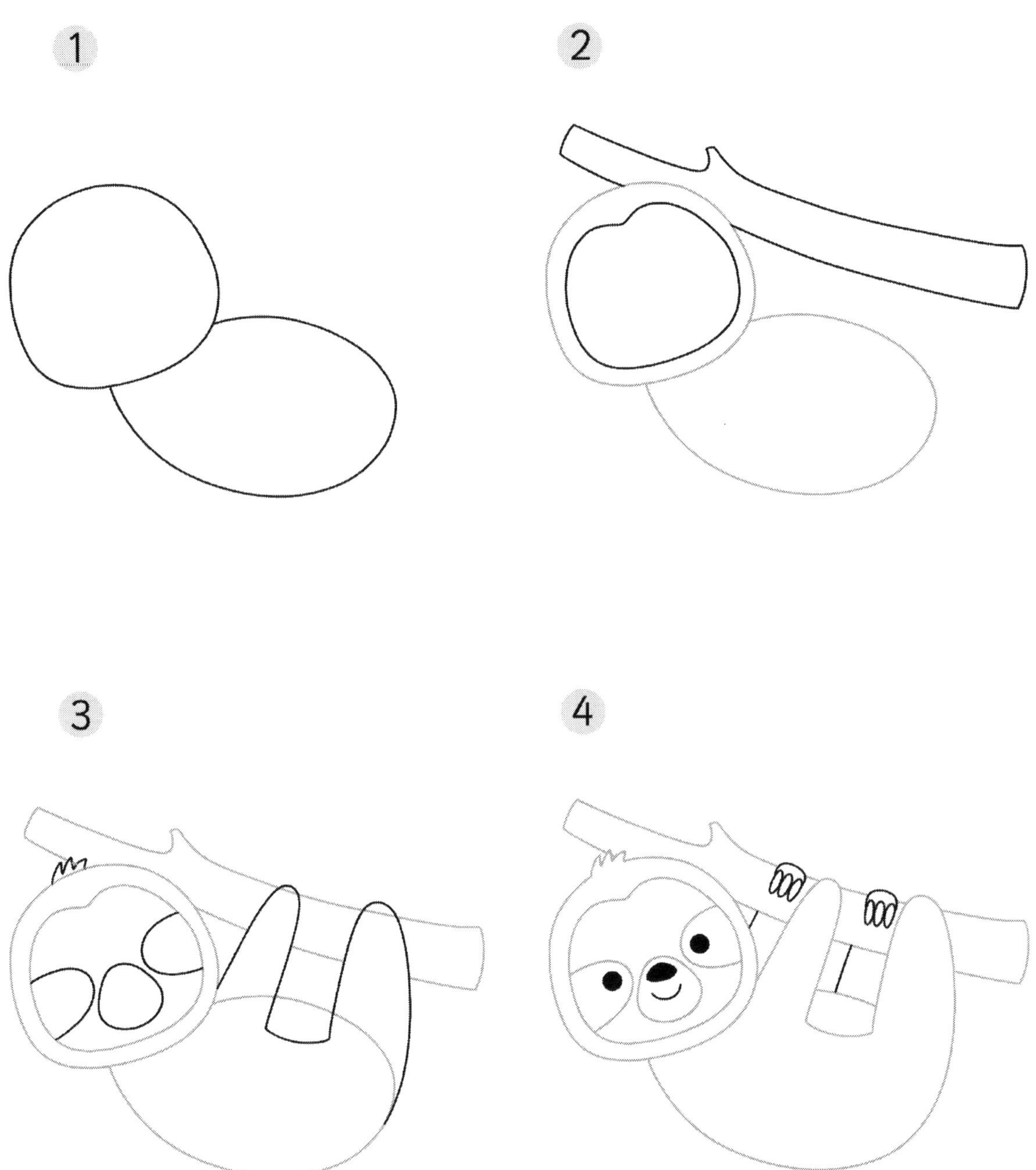

Trace along with me to practice

Now it's your turn on your own!

Parrot

Step-by-step instructions

1

2

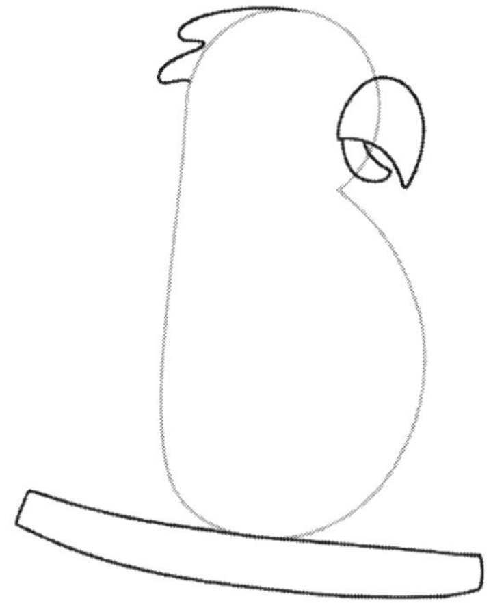

3

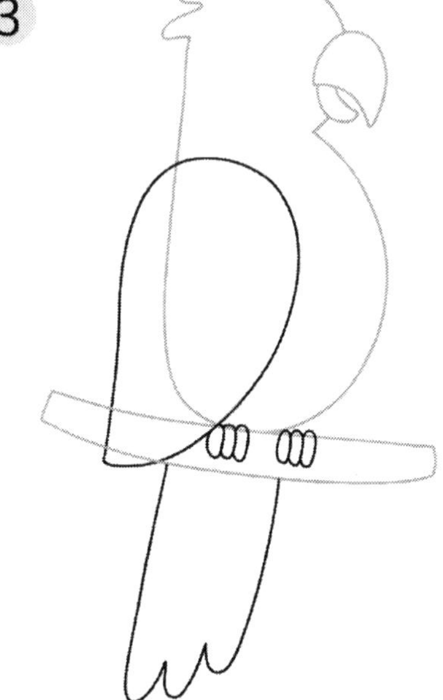

4

Trace along with me to practice

Now it's your turn on your own!

Gorilla

Step-by-step instructions

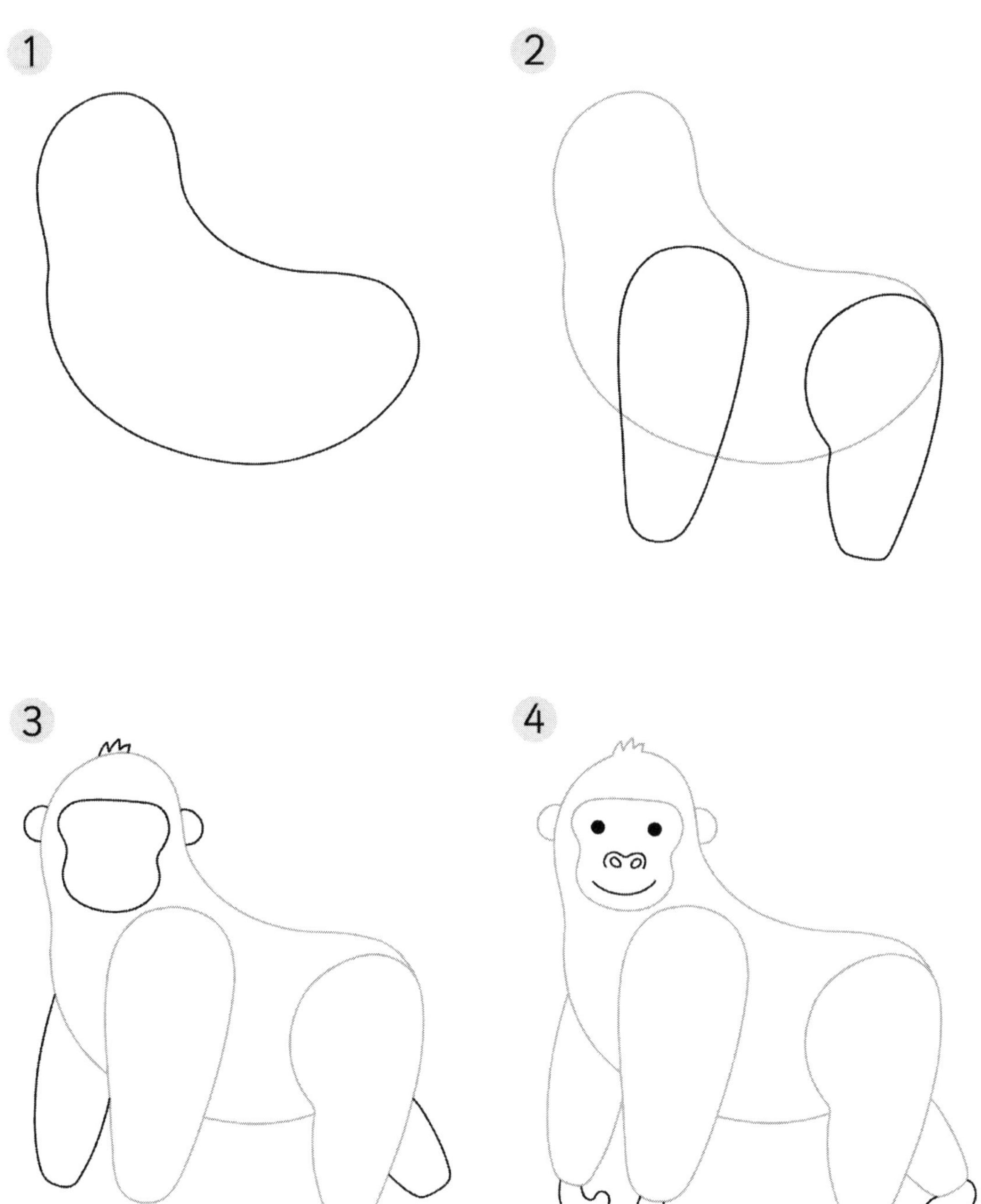

Trace along with me to practice

Now it's your turn on your own!

Snake

Step-by-step instructions

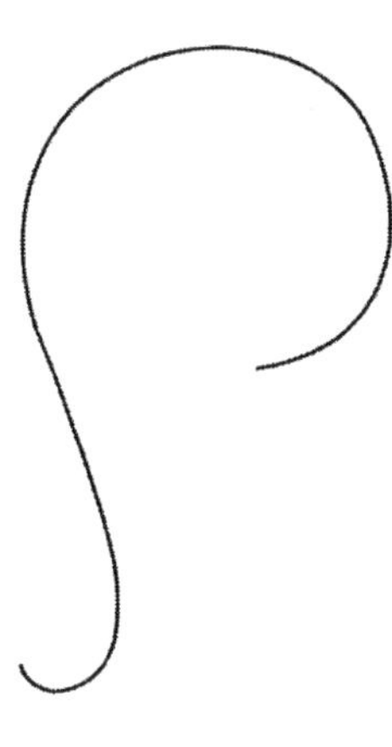

2

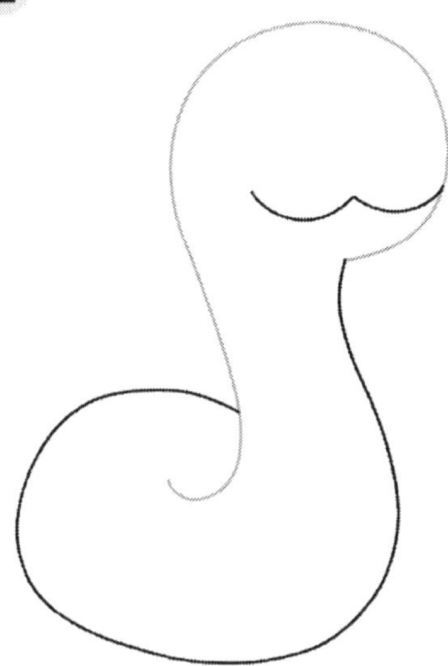

3

4

Trace along with me to practice

Now it's your turn on your own!

Iguana

Step-by-step instructions

1

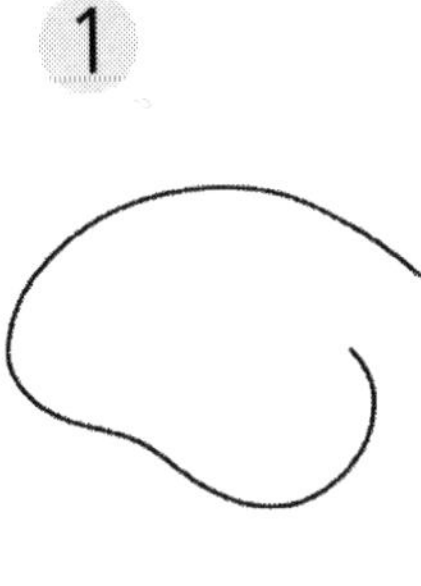

2

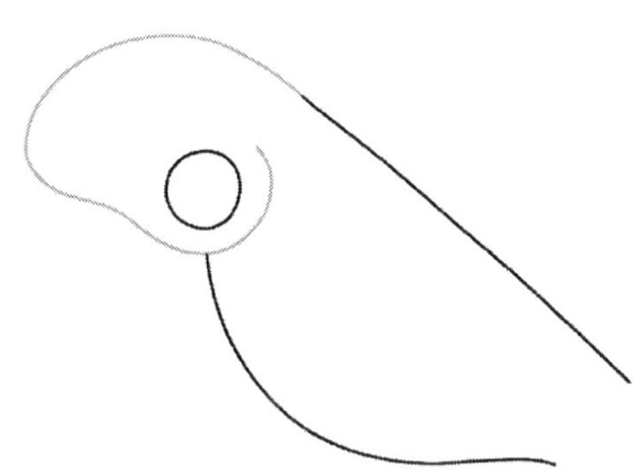

3

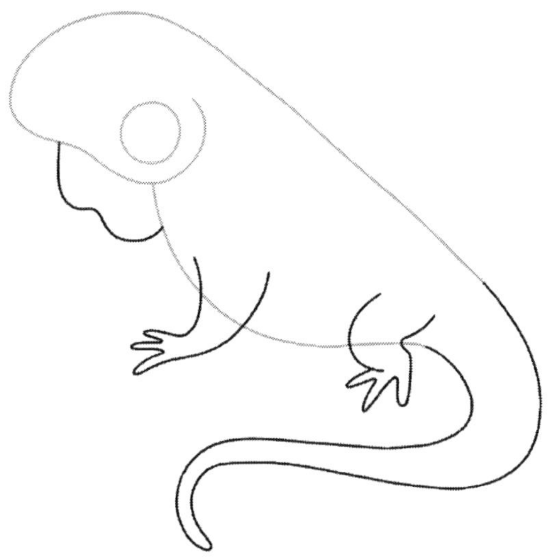

4

Trace along with me to practice

Now it's your turn on your own!

Toucan

Step-by-step instructions

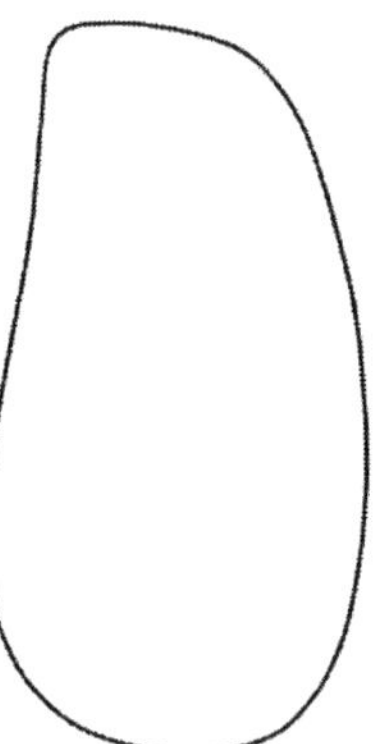

2

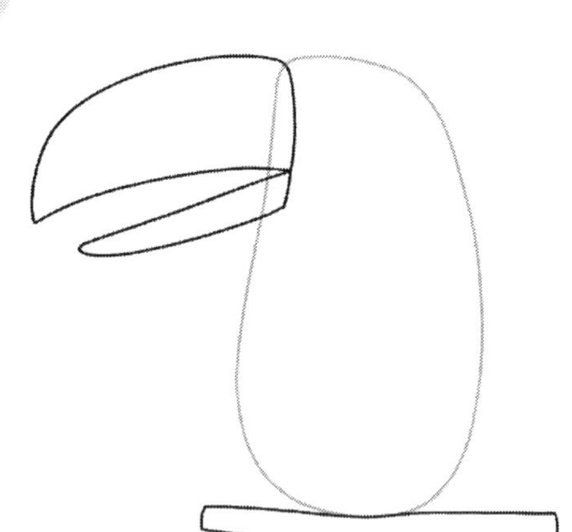

3

4

Trace along with me to practice

Now it's your turn on your own!

Lion

Step-by-step instructions

Trace along with me to practice

Now it's your turn on your own!

Giraffe

Step-by-step instructions

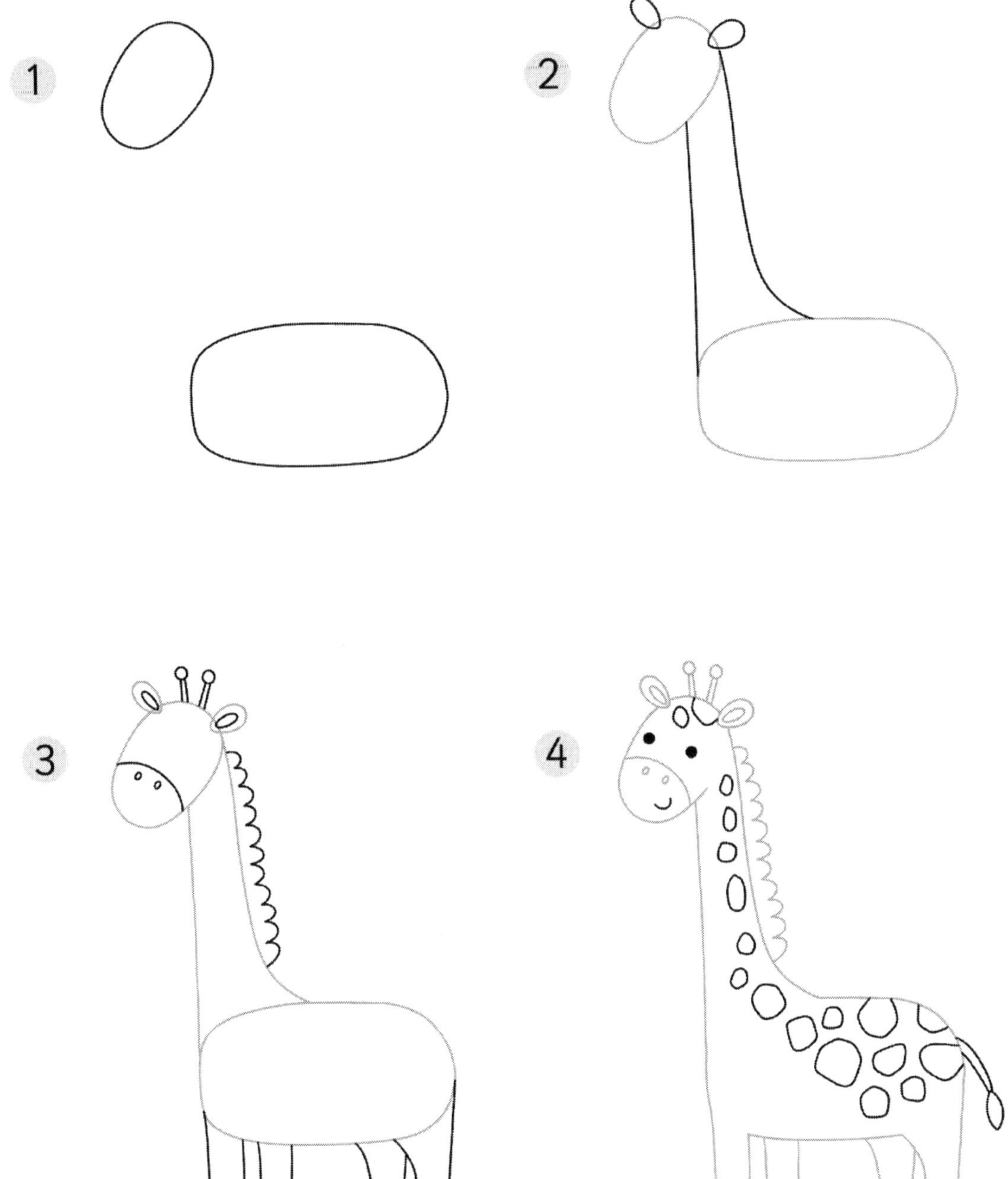

Trace along with me to practice

Now it's your turn on your own!

Rhinoceros

Step-by-step instructions

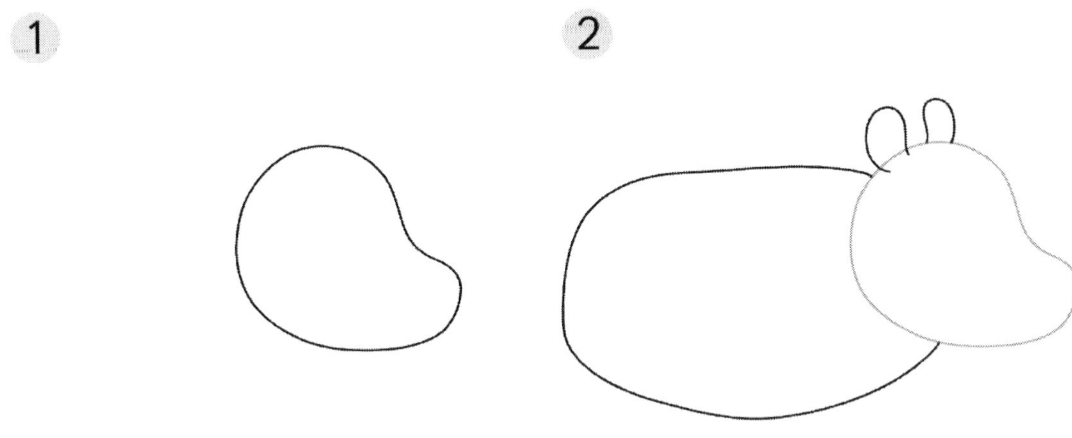

Trace along with me to practice

Now it's your turn on your own!

Zebra

Step-by-step instructions

Trace along with me to practice

Now it's your turn on your own!

Elephant

Step-by-step instructions

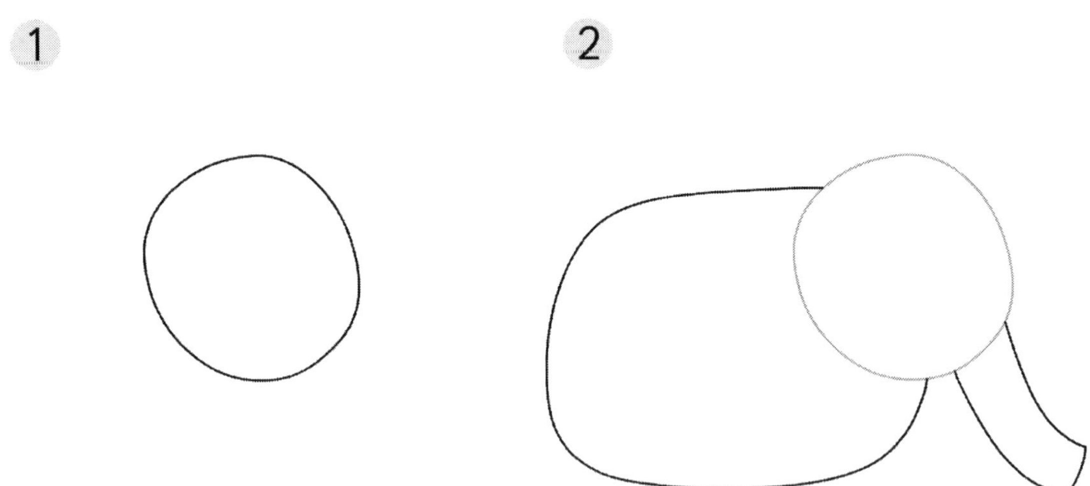

Trace along with me to practice

Now it's your turn on your own!

Cheetah

Step-by-step instructions

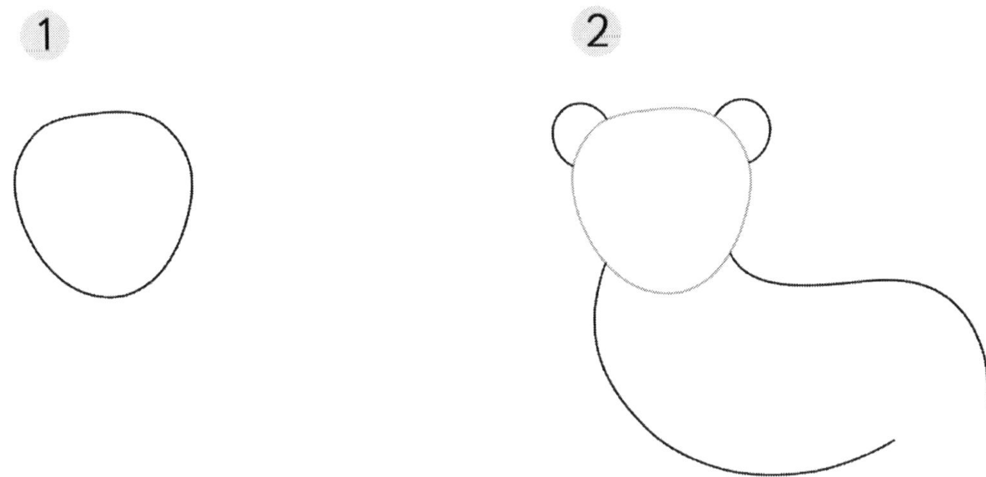

Trace along with me to practice

Now it's your turn on your own!

Crocodile

Step-by-step instructions

1 2

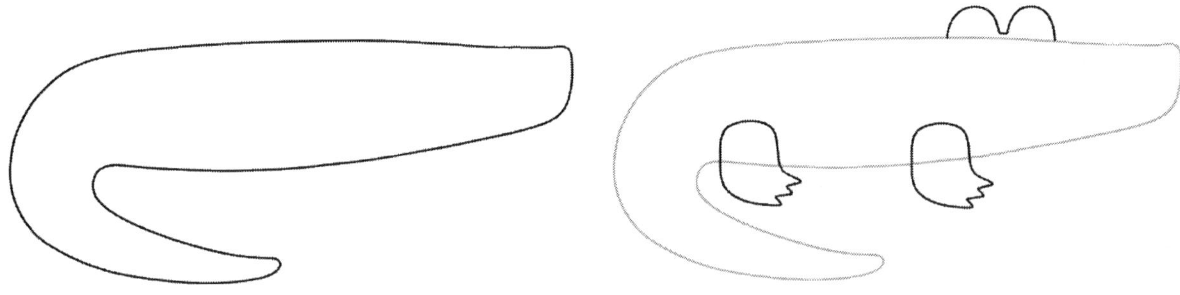

3 4

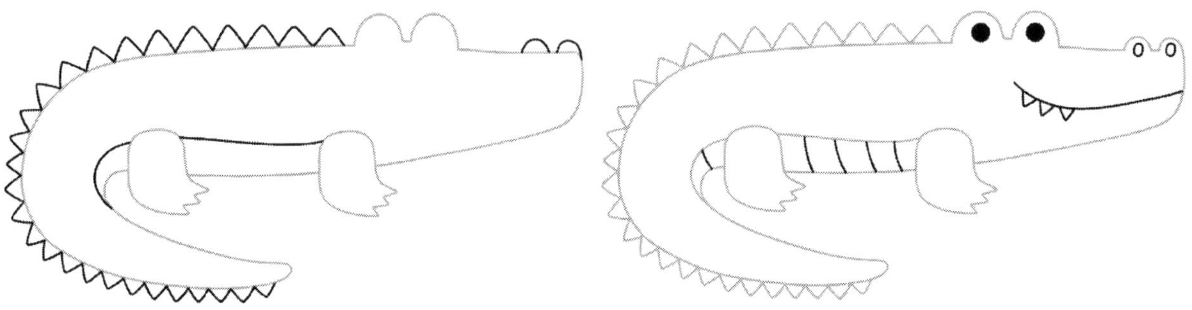

Trace along with me to practice

Now it's your turn on your own!

Flamingo

Step-by-step instructions

1

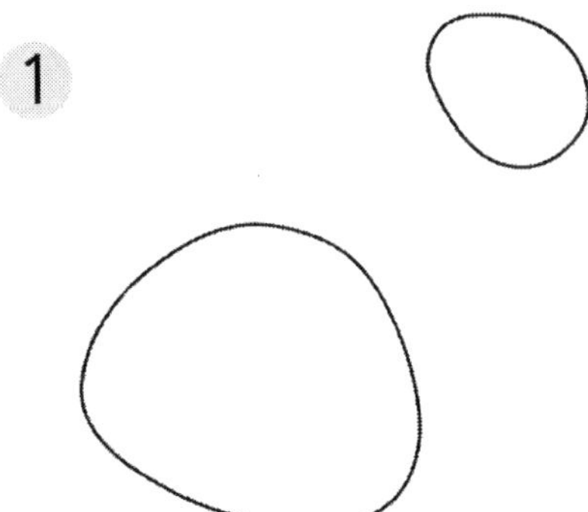

2

3

4

Trace along with me to practice

Now it's your turn on your own!

Hippopotamus

Step-by-step instructions

2

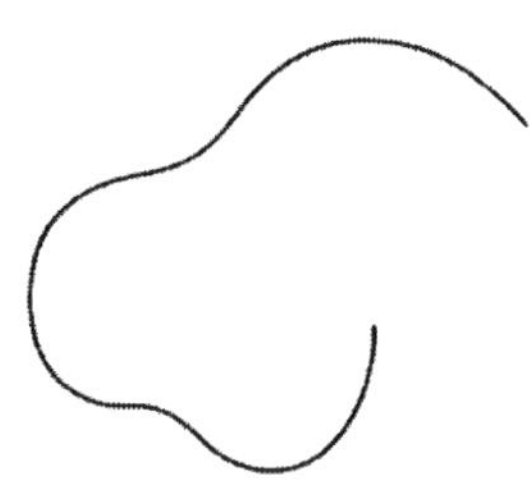

3

4

Trace along with me to practice

Now it's your turn on your own!

Ostrich

Step-by-step instructions

1

2

3

4

Trace along with me to practice

Now it's your turn on your own!

Shark

Step-by-step instructions

1

2

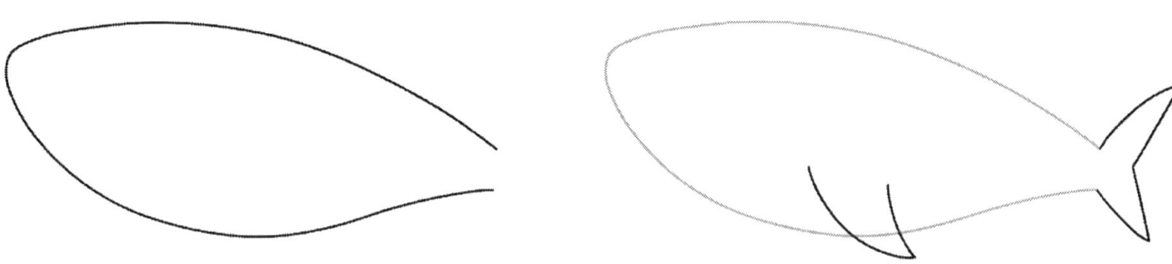

3

4

Trace along with me to practice

Now it's your turn on your own!

Penguin

Step-by-step instructions

1

2

3

4

Trace along with me to practice

Now it's your turn on your own!

Dolphin

Step-by-step instructions

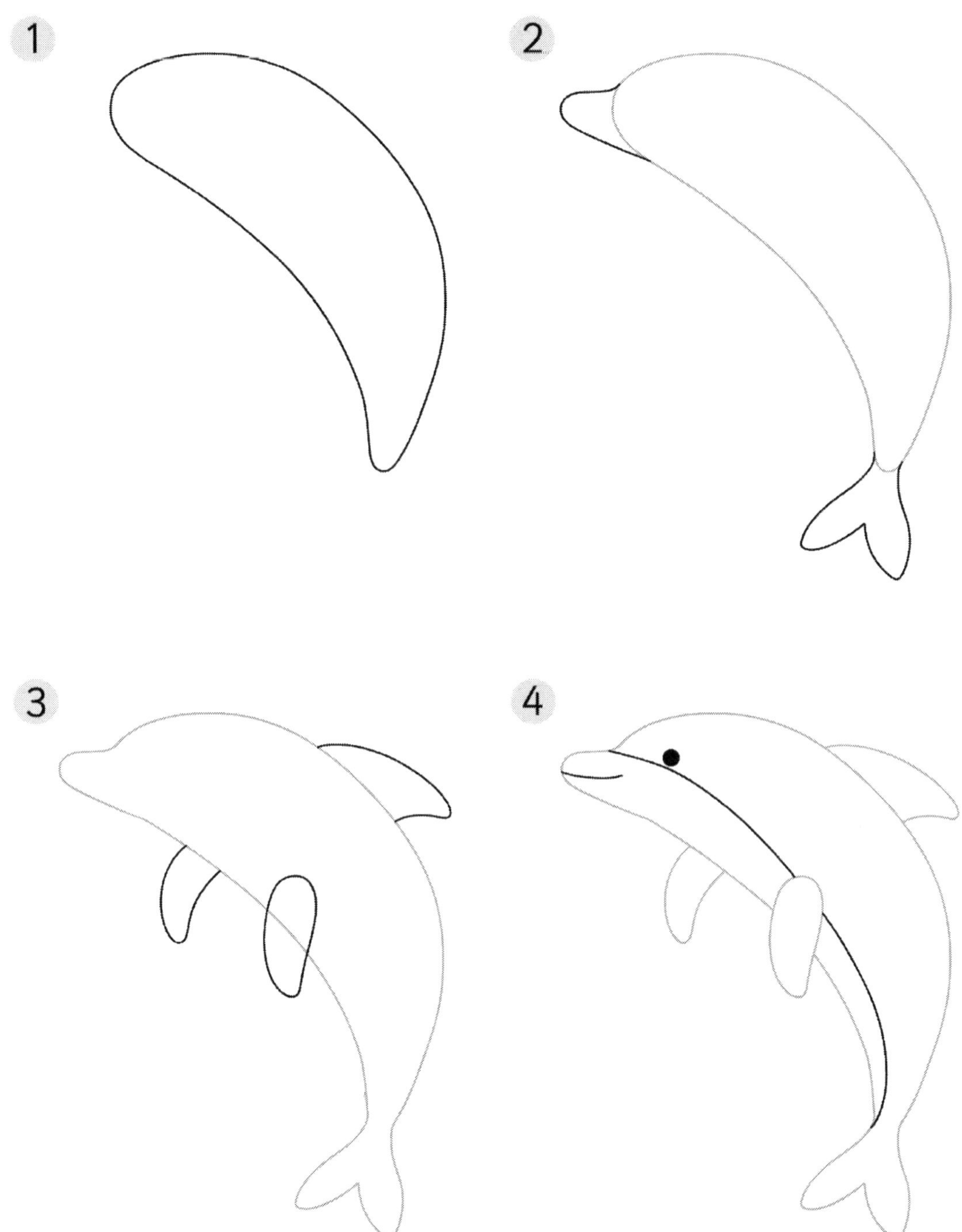

Trace along with me to practice

Now it's your turn on your own!

Fish

Step-by-step instructions

1

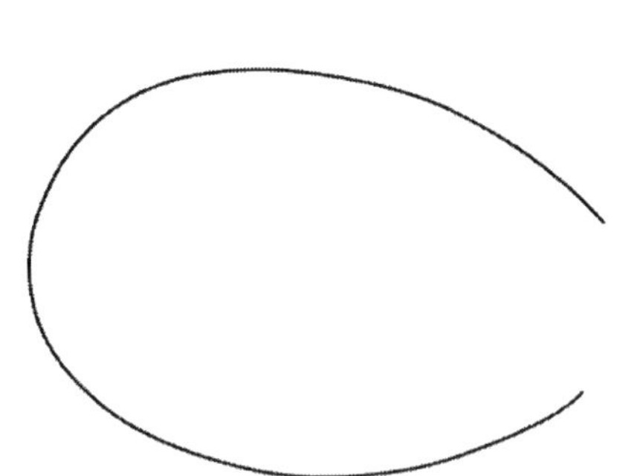

2

3

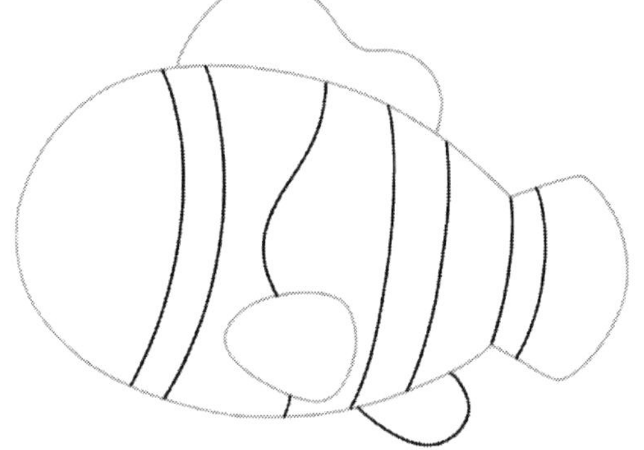

4

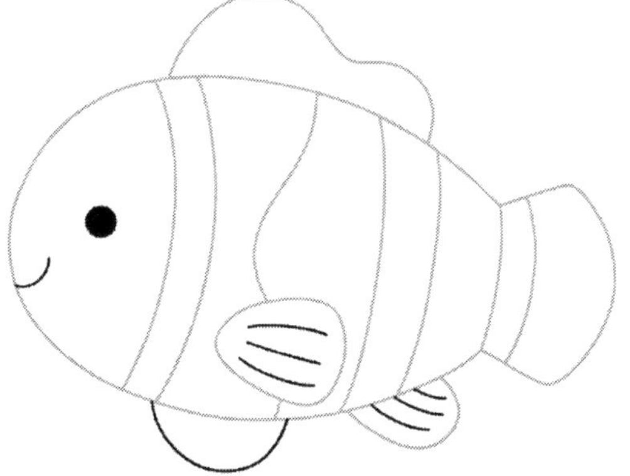

Trace along with me to practice

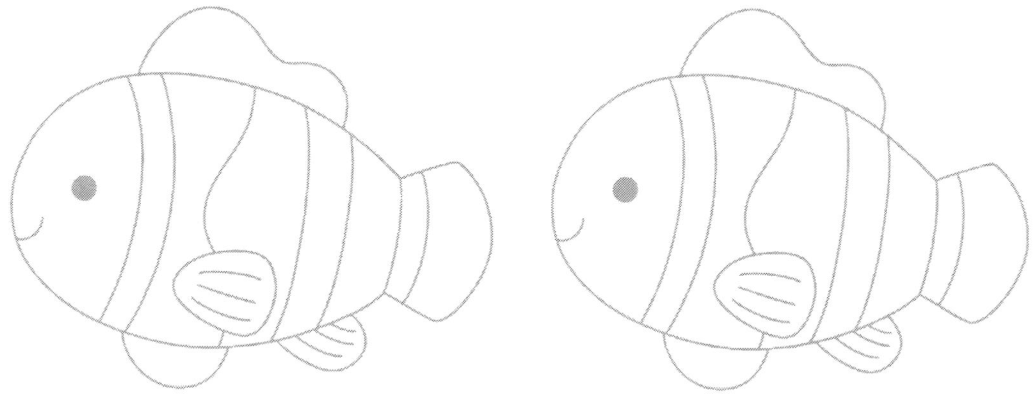

Now it's your turn on your own!

Stingray

Step-by-step instructions

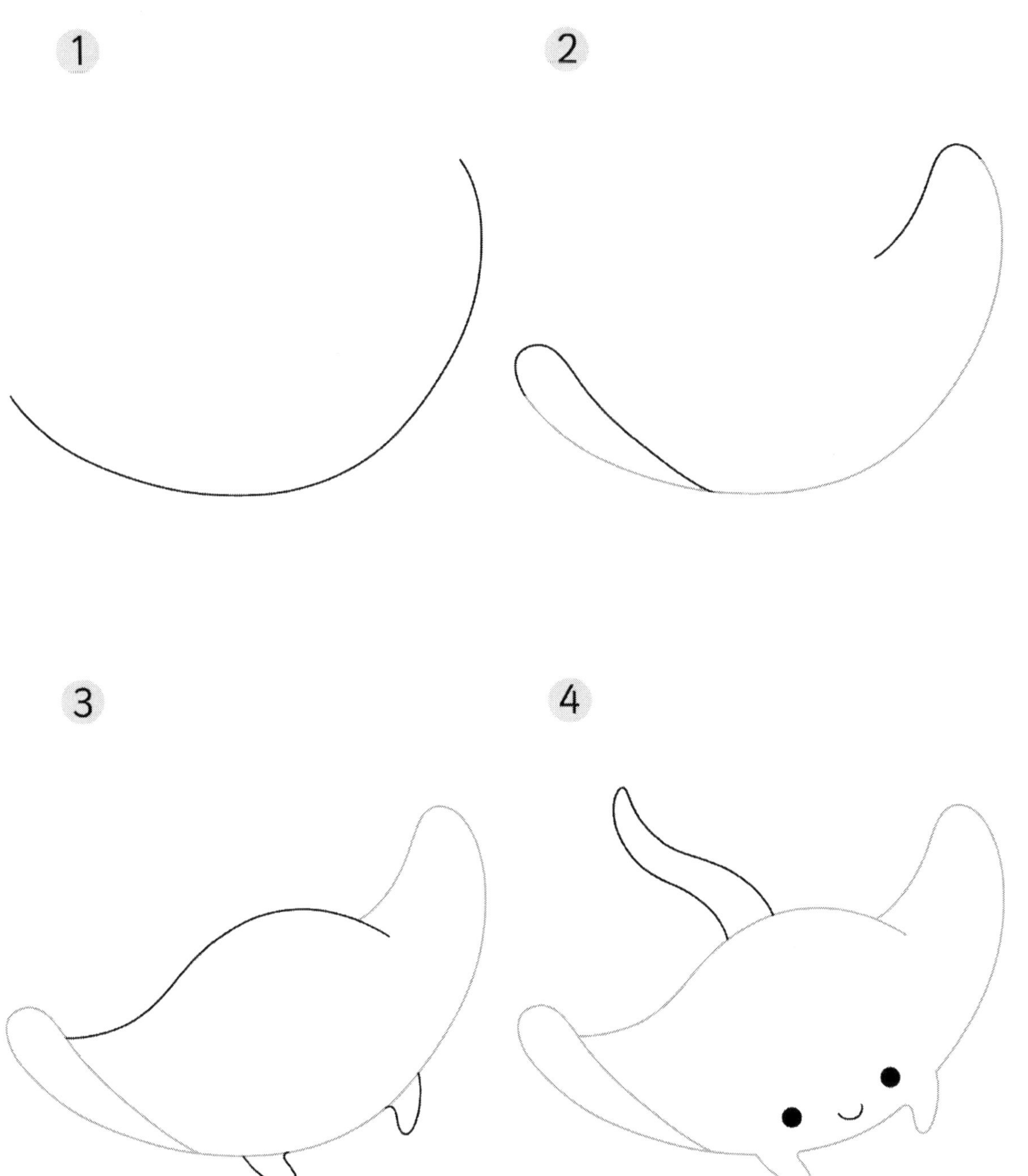

Trace along with me to practice

Now it's your turn on your own!

Otter

Step-by-step instructions

1

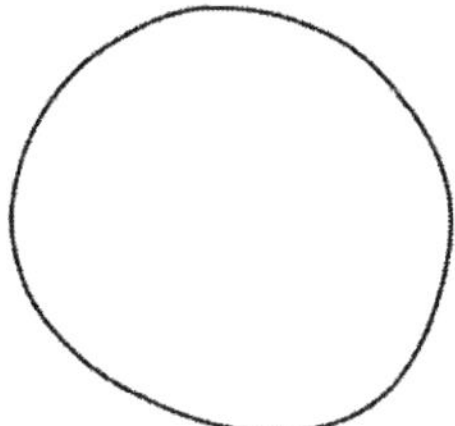

2

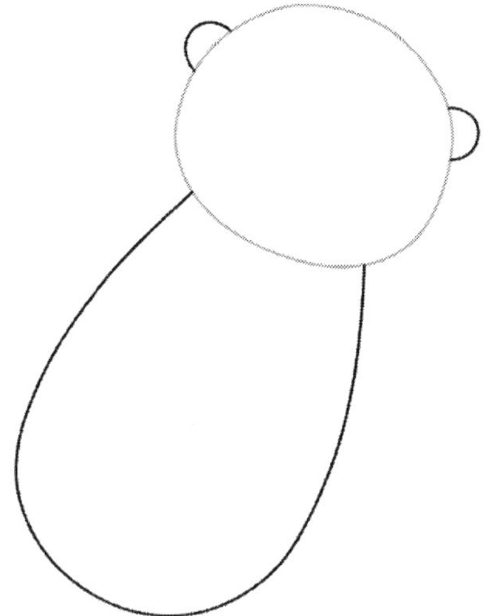

3

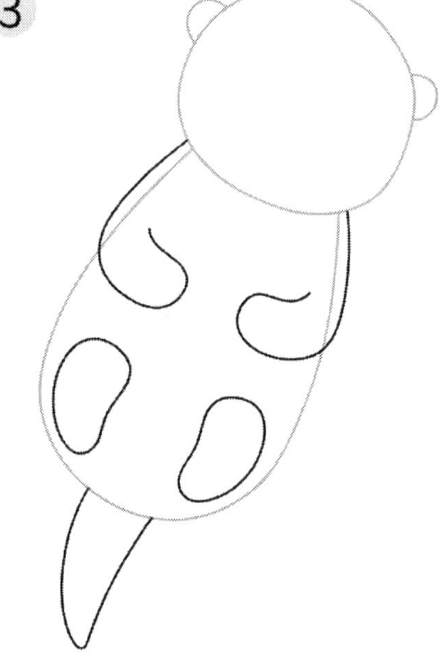

4

Trace along with me to practice

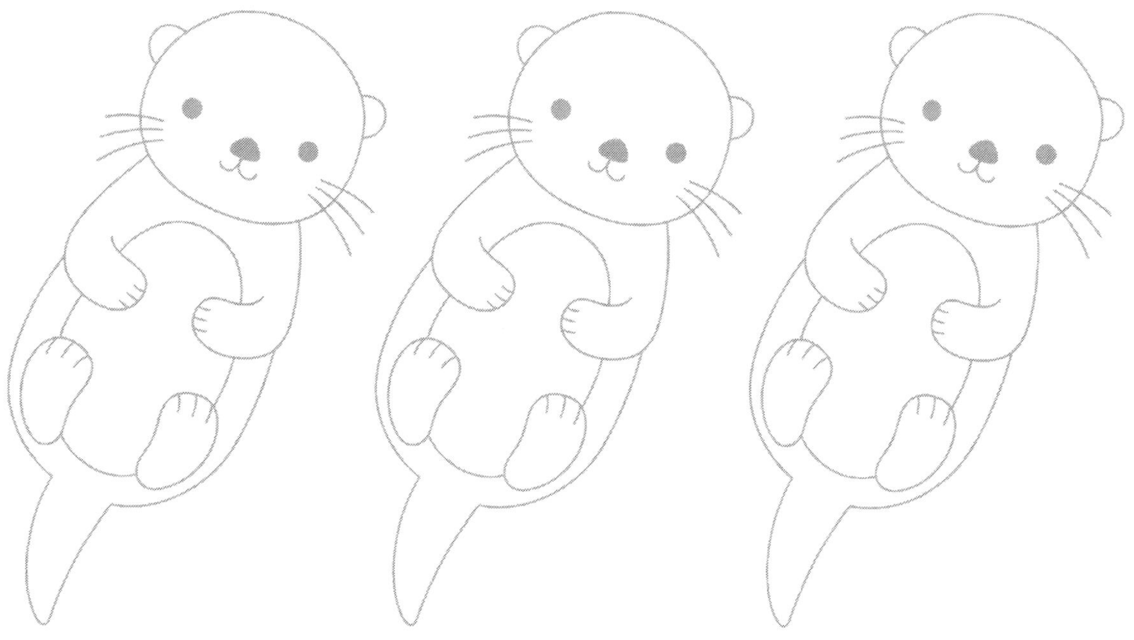

Now it's your turn on your own!

Octopus

Step-by-step instructions

1

2

3

4

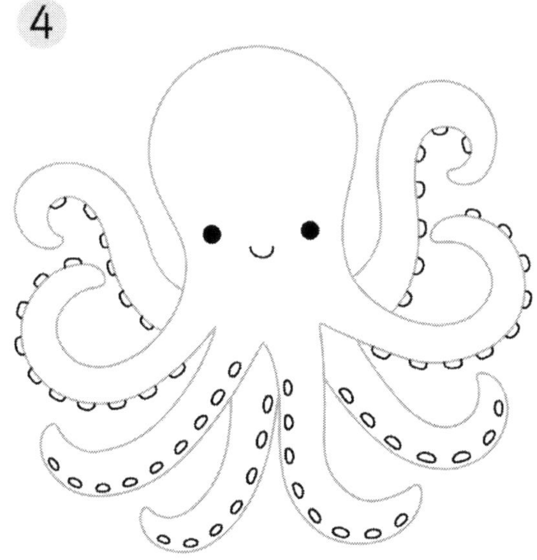

Trace along with me to practice

Now it's your turn on your own!

Orca

Step-by-step instructions

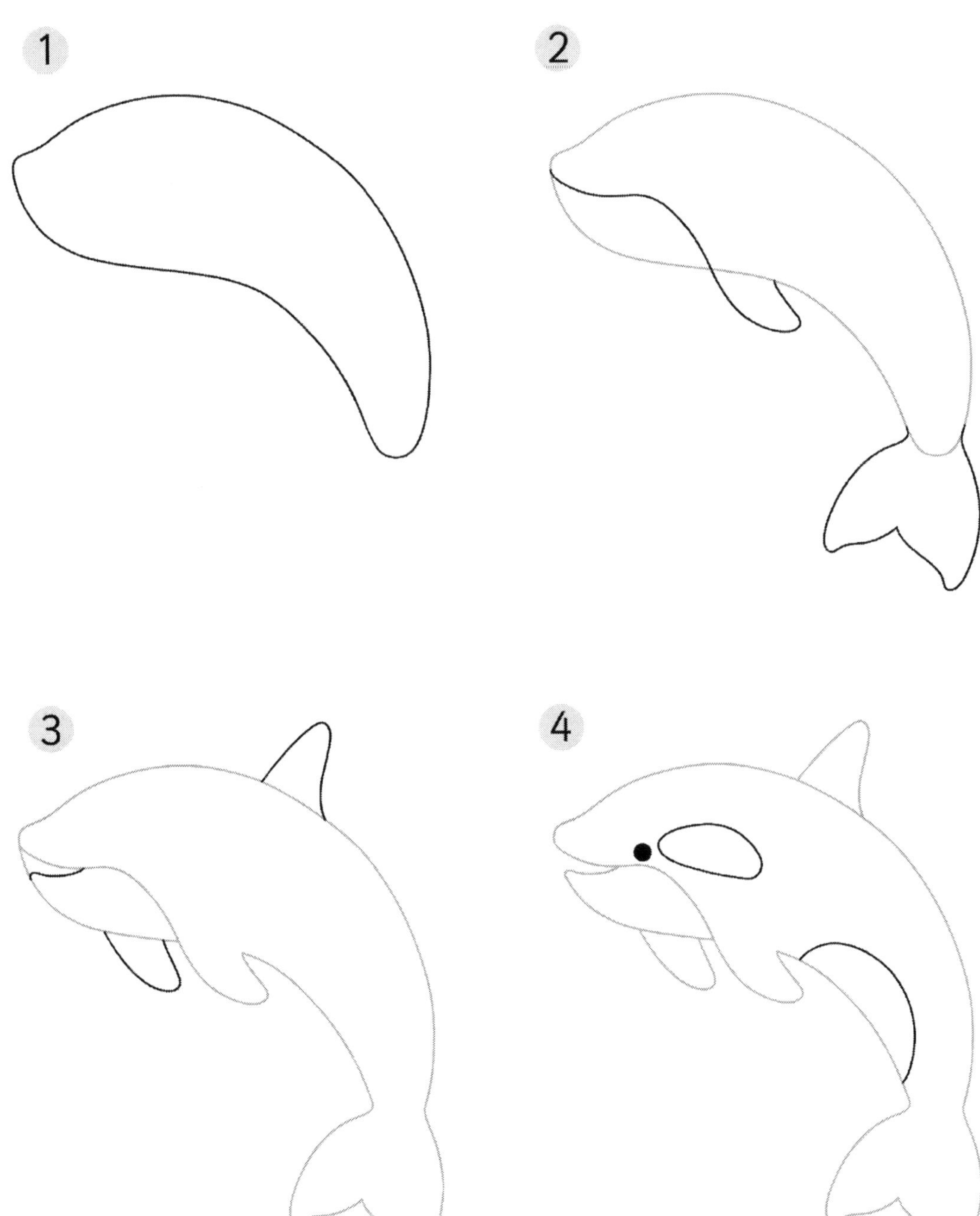

Trace along with me to practice

Now it's your turn on your own!

Walrus

Step-by-step instructions

2

3

4

Trace along with me to practice

Now it's your turn on your own!

The Littlest Press is a fun-size family-run publishing company with big dreams! We love to spread joy through fun and beautifully designed products that help kids learn and do new things.

Honest reviews from customers like you are so essential to our business and will help us to continue to make great products like this one.

Thank you for your feedback!

Follow us on Instagram for the latest on new releases and special giveaways:
@thelittlestpress

Made in the USA
Middletown, DE
25 July 2021